galerie
andresthalmann

Donald Sultan
Recent Work

Exhibition 23 October - 23 December 2009

Lantern Flowers July 30 2009 Enamel, tar and spackle on tile over wood, 30 x 30 cm

VORWORT *FOREWORD*

Donald Sultans Werke fesseln und begeistern den Betrachter durch ihre schlichte Schönheit und kraftvolle Intensität. Kürzlich durfte ich dies wieder erfahren als ich in seinem New Yorker Atelier vor den Werken stand, die er eigens für unsere Ausstellung geschaffen hat.

Mein herzlicher Dank geht an Donald Sultan für unsere Freundschaft und Zusammenarbeit seit 1996. Ich freue mich sehr, seine jüngsten Werke in meiner Galerie zu präsentieren. Ich hoffe, mit dieser Ausstellung meine Begeisterung für diesen bedeutenden amerikanischen Gegenwartskünstler auch an Sie weitergeben zu können.

Viewers are fascinated and arrested by the stark beauty and powerful intensity of Donald Sultan's works.
I realized this again during a recent visit to the artist at his studio in New York, where I saw the pieces specially created for our exhibition.

I am deeply grateful to Donald Sultan for his friendship and cooperation in all the years since 1996. And it is with great pleasure that I present his most recent works at my gallery. I trust that you will share my enthusiasm for this significant contemporary American artist.

Carina Andres Thalmann
Galerie Andres Thalmann

Donald Sultan - Recent Work

Donald Sultan transformiert die Intimität der Stillleben-malerei in wuchtige Plastizität. Auf massiven Bildträgern sind Blumen oder Gegenstände in pechschwarzem Teer eingelassen. Die gesättigte Schwärze des Bildgrunds unterstreicht die Fragilität des Ephemeren und erzeugt gleichsam eine sogartige Bildwirkung.

Die „Lantern-Paintings" sind in der Manier der Pop Art grossflächig und mit klar umrissenen Konturen gemalt. In ihrer vereinheitlichenden Stilisierung werden die Windlichter gleichsam zum Emblem geadelt, das sich durch den harten Farbkontrast dezidiert vom Bildgrund abhebt. Bei den „Lantern Flowers" nimmt Sultan die Farbe zurück. Die Motive heben sich einzig durch den Glanz des Emails vom matten Grund ab und eröffnen so ein ambivalentes Wechselspiel – ein „push" und „pull" zwischen Vorder- und Hintergrund.

Donald Sultan ersetzt die traditionellen Malutensilien – den Pinsel, Pigmente und die Leinwand – mit industriellen Materialien. Um seiner Malerei Körperlichkeit zu verleihen, tüftelte Sultan in den siebziger Jahren eine entsprechende Technik aus. Mittlerweile ist sie zum Markenzeichen seiner Kunst geworden. Aus Holzfaserplatten konstruiert er ein Gerüst, verkleidet es mit Linoleumplatten und überzieht es anschliessend mit Teer. Dann schneidet er mit einem Messer oder Lötkolben seine Motive aus der Teerschicht heraus. Die Negativformen füllt er mit Spachtelmasse und trägt darauf die Farbe oder eine dünne Lage von Email auf. Bei einzelnen Serien wird die Farbschicht schliesslich im Siebdruckverfahren bedruckt.

Der rohe Bildgrund, den Sultan als „something brutal and beginning" bezeichnet, steht in spannungsvollem Gegensatz zu den fein ausgearbeiteten Bildflächen. Der Künstler entwickelte seine Arbeitsweise im Kontext der Process Art und der Pop Art, die in New York in den siebziger Jahren dominierten. Sultans Werke können gleichsam als Verquickung dieser Kunstrichtungen gelesen werden. So kombiniert er kunstfremde Materialien und Verfahren mit stilistischen und ikonographischen Strategien der Pop Art.

Sultans Repertoire umfasst neben klassischen Stilllebenmotiven wie Blumen und Früchte auch banale Gebrauchsgegenstände. Die umfangreiche Serie über die Zitrone, die oft zentriert auf schwarzem Grund disponiert ist, wurde in der Kunstwelt aufgrund ihrer ambivalenten Umsetzung rege rezipiert. Die Konturen der Frucht – ein praller Körper mit wohlgeformten Spitzen – weisen symbolische Komponenten auf. In farblichen Variationen werden die Zitronen zuweilen als schwarze Objekte gezeigt. Dies verdeutlicht, dass der Bildgegenstand für den Maler wesentlich als malerisches, gestalterisches Element von Bedeutung ist.

Donald Sultan ist bislang der jüngste Künstler, der mit 37 Jahren im Museum of Modern Art in New York mit einer Einzelausstellung gewürdigt wurde. Die Sammlungen zahlreicher renommierter Institutionen – u.a. das Museum of Modern Art, das Dallas Museum of Art und das Metropolitan Museum of Art – enthalten Werke von Donald Sultan. Im Jahre 2008 kam unter dem Titel „Donald Sultan: The Theater of the Object" eine Monografie über seine 30-jährige Künstlerkarriere heraus. In der Galerie Andres Thalmann präsentiert er ausgewählte Arbeiten aus seinen jüngsten Werkserien.

Ruth Littman
Leiterin Galerie Andres Thalmann

Donald Sultan Fotografie: Phyllis Rose

Donald Sultan - Recent Work

Donald Sultan has transformed the intimacy of still-life paintings into weighty plasticity. Flowers or other objects seem to float on his sculptural, pitch-black tar supports. The saturated blackness of the ground not only emphasises the fragility of the ephemeral, it also produces an undercurrent that seems to pull the viewer in.

The bold colours, hard contours and stylization of Sultan's Lantern Paintings are reminiscent of Pop Art; the stark colour contrasts in the lantern motifs elevate them to emblematic status. Colours are more muted in Sultan's Lantern Flowers, where it is only the enamel gloss that distinguishes the motifs from the matte ground, producing an ambivalent interplay – a push and pull between foreground and background.

Donald Sultan substitutes industrial materials for more traditional ones such as brush, pigments and canvas. A technique devised in the 1970s to render his paintings more physical has since become his brand mark: he covers thick Masonite panels with linoleum, which he smears with tar. Then he proceeds to cut out his motifs using a knife or soldering iron before filling the negative forms with spackling paste, and applying paint or a thin coat of enamel to the motifs only. In some of his series, the works are finished off with an application of screen-printing. The raw ground that Sultan describes as „something brutal and beginning" provides an exciting contrast to the painstakingly elaborated motifs.

The artist developed his technique in the context of Process and Pop Art that dominated the 1970s New York art world. His works may be interpreted as a blending of the two movements, for example when he combines materials and processes unrelated to art with the stylistic and iconographic strategies of Pop Art.

Sultan's repertoire covers the classical still-life motifs of fruit and flowers, but also includes objects of everyday use. His large series of lemons, ambivalent in their execution and often centrally depicted on black, caused a stir in the art scene. There is clearly a symbolic hint in the sensual contours and well-defined tips of the fruits. Occasionally, the lemons are depicted as black objects, as if to emphasize their compositional relevance.

He was only 37 when the Museum of Modern Art in New York honoured his oeuvre by presenting a solo show of his Black Lemons. His works feature in the permanent collections of many prestigious institutions, including The Museum of Modern Art, the Dallas Museum of Art, and the Metropolitan Museum of Art. A monograph of Sultan's 30-year career entitled „Donald Sultan: The Theater of the Object" was published in 2008. The Andres Thalmann Gallery is proud to present a selection from his most recent series.

Ruth Littman
Director, Andres Thalmann Gallery

Red Lanterns July 24 2007 Enamel, screenprint, tar and spackle on tile over masonite, 122 x 122 cm

Nine Lanterns Aug 22 2007   Enamel, screenprint, tar and spackle on tile over masonite, 91 x 91 cm

Lantern Flowers Sept 28 2009 Tar and spackle on tile over masonite, 91 x 91 cm

Lantern Flowers Oct 1 2009   Enamel, tar and spackle on tile over masonite, 91 x 91 cm

Lantern Flowers Aug 28 2009 Enamel, tar and spackle on tile over wood, 30 x 30 cm

Liquid Blacks July 10 2009 Enamel, tar and spackle on tile over masonite, 244 x 244 cm

Black and Blue April 11 2009   Enamel, tar and spackle on tile over masonite, 61 x 61 cm

Blues and Blacks Jan 20 2005 Enamel, tar and spackle on tile over masonite, 91 x 91 cm

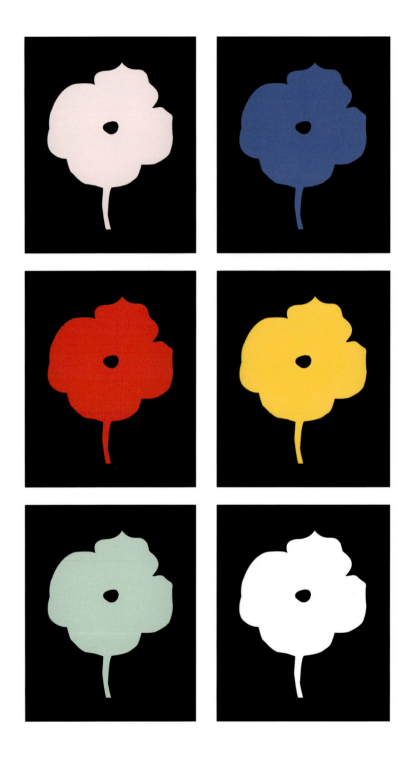

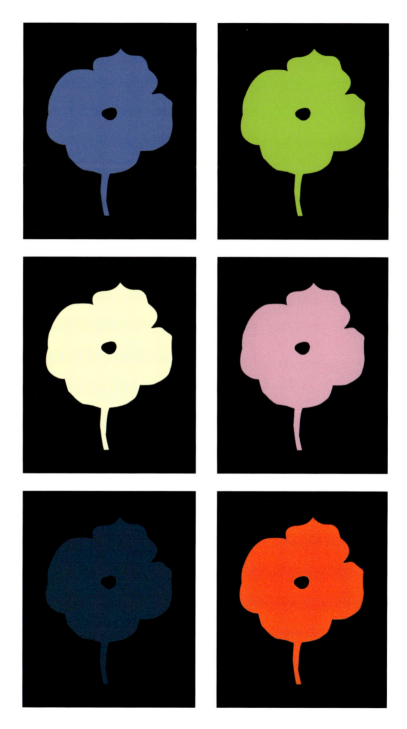

12 Colors March 13 2007 Silkscreen, set of 12 prints, each 64 x 51 cm

Yellow Mimosa Oct 1 2009 Conté, charcoal and flock on paper, 50 x 70 cm

Mimosa Feb 19 2009 Conté and graphite on paper, 69 x 100 cm

Mimosa July 31 2009 Conté, graphite and ink on paper, 69 x 100 cm

Mimosa Sept 16 2009 Conté and charcoal on paper, 69 x 100 cm

Mimosa July 23 2009 Conté and graphite on paper, 69 x 100 cm

Mimosa April 16 2009 Conté and graphite on paper, 50 x 70 cm

BIOGRAPHY

1951	Born, Asheville, North Carolina.
1973	BFA, University of North Carolina, Chapel Hill.
1975	MFA, School of the Art Institute, Chicago.
1978-79	Creative Artists Public Service Grant, New York.
1980-81	State National Endowment for the Arts.
2000	Awarded an honorary doctorate degree from the Corcoran School of Art, Washington D.C.
2002	Awarded an honorary doctorate degree from the New York Academy of Art, NY.
2007	Awarded an honorary doctorate degree from the University of North Carolina, Asheville

A SELECTION OF SOLO-EXHIBITIONS

1977	Artists Space, New York, New York.
	The Institute of the Art and Urban Resources, P.S. 1 Special Projects Room, Long Island City, New York.
1979	Willard Gallery, New York, New York.
	Young Hoffman Gallery, Chicago, Illinois.
1980	Willard Gallery, New York, New York.
1981	Weinberg Gallery, San Francisco, California.
1982	Blum Helman Gallery, New York, New York.
	Hans Strelow Gallery, Dusseldorf, Germany.
1983	Akira Ikeda Gallery, Tokyo, Japan. Catalogue.
1984	Blum Helman Gallery, New York, New York.
1985	Blum Helman Gallery, New York, New York.
	Blum Helman Gallery, New York, New York.
	Gian Enzo Sperone, Rome, Italy. Catalogue.
	Traveling exhibition: "Donald Sultan: Prints 1979-1985":
	Barbara Krakow Gallery, Boston, MA.
	Georgia State University, Atlanta.
	Baxter Gallery, Portland School of Art, Maine.
	Wesleyan University, Middletown, CT.
	Asheville Art Museum, Asheville, NC.
	California State University, Long Beach.
1986	Blum Helman Gallery, New York, New York.
	A.P. Giannini Gallery, Bank of America, World Headquarters, San Francisco, California.
	Galerie Montenay-Delsol, Paris, France.
	Galerie de l'Estampe Contemporaine Bibliothèque Nationale, Paris.
	The Greenberg Gallery, St. Louis, Missouri.
	Blum Helman Gallery, Los Angeles, California.
1987	Akira Ikeda Gallery, Nagoya, Japan.
	Blum Helman Gallery, New York, New York.
	Barbara Krakow Gallery, Boston, MA.
	Gian Enzo Sperone Gallery, Rome, Italy.
	Greg Kucera Gallery, Seattle, Washington.
	University Art Museum, Long Beach, CA.
	Traveling exhibition: "Donald Sultan: Cigarette Paintings 1980-81, Photographs 1985-86":
	Blum Helman Gallery, New York, New York.
	Blum Helman Gallery, Los Angeles, California.
	Traveling exhibition: "Donald Sultan":
	Museum of Contemporary Art, Chicago, Illinois.
	Los Angeles Museum of Contemporary Art, CA.
	Fort Worth Art Museum, Texas.
	Brooklyn Museum, New York. Catalogue.
1988	Museum of Modern Art, New York, New York: "Donald Sultan's Black Lemons".
	Galerie Montenay, Paris, France.
	La Galerie Alice Pauli, Lausanne, Switzerland.
	Marina Hamilton Gallery, New York, New York.
1989	Blum Helman Gallery, Santa Monica, California.
	Paul Kasmin Gallery, Inc., New York, New York.
	Runkle-Hue-Williams, Ltd., London, England.
	The Greenberg Gallery, St. Louis, Missouri.
	Knoedler & Co., New York, New York.
	Richard Green Gallery, New York, New York.
1990	Knoedler & Company, New York, New York.
	Greg Kucera Gallery, Seattle, Washington.
	Equinox Gallery, Vancouver, Canada.
	Waddington Galleries, London, England.
1991	Berggruen Gallery, San Francisco, California.
	Knoedler & Company, New York, New York.
	Mary Ryan Gallery, New York, New York.
	Meredith Long Gallery, Houston, Texas.
	Greg Kucera Gallery, Seattle, Washington.
	Richard Green Gallery, Santa Monica, CA.
1992	The Hill Gallery, Birmingham, Michigan.
	Knoedler & Company, New York, New York.
	Galeria Trauma, Barcelona, Spain. Catalogue.
	Hans Strelow Gallery, Dusseldorf, Germany.
	Meredith Long & Company, Houston, Texas.
	Guild Hall Museum, East Hampton, New York.
	Knoedler & Company, New York, New York..
	Traveling exhibition: The American Federation of the Arts, New York, New York (organizing and circulating institution): "Donald Sultan: A Print Retrospective," Curated by Barry Walker:
	Lowe Art Museum, University of Miami, Coral Gables, Florida, 1992.
	Butler Institute of American Art, Youngstown, Ohio.

Museum of Fine Arts, Houston, Texas, 1993.
Sheldon Memorial Art Gallery, University of Nebraska, Lincoln, 1994.
Madison Art Center, Wisconsin, 1994.
Orlando Museum of Art, Florida, 1994.
Memphis Brooks Museum of Art, Tennessee, 1995.

1993 Galerie Kaj Forsblom, Zurich, Switzerland.
Hill Gallery, Birmingham, Michigan.
Knoedler & Company, New York, New York.

1994 Galeria 56, Budapest, Hungary.
Paul Kasmin Gallery, New York, New York.
Jaffe Baker Blau, Boca Raton, Florida.

1995 Knoedler & Company, New York, New York.
Hill Gallery, Birmingham, Michigan.
Asheville Art Museum, North Carolina.

1996 Baldwin Gallery, Aspen, Colorado.
Meredith Long & Company, Houston, Texas.
Fotouhi Cramer Gallery, East Hampton, New York.
Galerie Lawrence Rubin, Zurich, Switzerland.
Mary Ryan Gallery, New York, New York.
Paul Kasmin Gallery, New York, New York.
Guild Hall, East Hampton, New York: Exhibition in conjunction with the Hampton's International Film Festival.

1997 Knoedler & Co, New York, New York.
Greenberg Van Doren Gallery, St. Louis, Missouri.
Hill Gallery, Birmingham, Missouri.
Galerie Daniel Templon, Paris, France.
Janet Borden, Inc, New York, New York.

1998 Galerie Lutz and Thalmann. Zurich, Switzerland.
Baldwin Gallery - Aspen, Colorado.
Turner & Runyon Gallery, Dallas Texas.
Galleria Lawrence Rubin, Milano, Italy.

1999 The Jewish Museum - New York, New York.
Meredith Long & Co., Houston.
Knoedler - New York, New York.
Hill Gallery, Birmingham, Michigan.

2000 Hill Gallery, Birmingham, Michigan.
Cheekwood Museum of Art, Nashville, Tennessee.
Winston Wachter Fine Art, Seattle, Washington.
Galerie Simonne Stern, New Orleans, Louisiana.
Meredith Long Gallery, Houston, Texas.
Mary Ryan Gallery, New York, New York.
Traveling exhibition: "Donald Sultan: In the Still-Life Tradition":
Memphis Brooks Museum of Art, Memphis, TN.
Corcoran Gallery of Art, Washington, D.C.
Kemper Museum of Contemporary Art, Kansas City, Missouri.
Polk Museum of Art, Lakeland, Florida.
Scottsdale Museum of Contemporary Art, Scottsdale, Arizona.

2001 Baldwin Gallery, Aspen, Colorado.
Dorothy Blau Gallery, Bay Harbor Islands, FL.
Stephen F. Austin State University, Nacogdoches, Texas.
Raab Galerie, Berlin, Germany.
University of Michigan, Ann Arbor, Michigan.
Hill Gallery, Birmingham, Michigan.
Galerie Lutz and Thalmann, Zurich.
Lowe Gallery, Atlanta, Georgia.

2002 Imago Galleries, Palm Desert, California.
Louise Cameron Wells Art Museum, Wilmington, North Carolina.
Winston Wachter Fine Art, Seattle, Washington.

2003 Knoedler & Company, New York, New York.
Mary Ryan Gallery, New York, New York.
Galerie Forsblom, Helsinki, Finland.

2004 Meredith Long Gallery, Houston.
Singapore Tyler Print Institute, Singapore.
Ameringer & Yohe Fine Art, New York.

2005 Baldwin Gallery, Aspen, Colorado.
Cliff Lede Vineyards, Yountville, California.

2006 Centre Cultural Contemporani Pelaires, Mallorca, Spain. Catalogue.
Galerie Forsblom, Helsinki, Finland.

2007 Mary Ryan Gallery, New York, New York.
De Brock Gallery, Knokke-Heist, Belgium.
Meredith Long Gallery, Houston, Texas.

2008 Baldwin Gallery, Aspen, Colorado.
Aidan Gallery, Moscow, Russia.
Forsblom Projects, Helsinki, Finland.

2009 Mary Ryan Gallery, New York, New York.
Contemporary Arts Center, Cincinnati, Ohio.
Greenfield-Sacks Gallery, Santa Monica, CA.
Galerie Ernst Hilger, Vienna, Austria.
Ben Brown Fine Arts, London, England.
Galerie Andres Thalmann, Zurich, Switzerland.

EXHIBITION CATALOGUES (SELECTION)

TUCKER, MARCIA: „FOUR ARTISTS: DRAWINGS". THE NEW MUSEUM, NEW YORK, 1977.

RUSH, DAVID: „CONTEMPORARY DRAWING - NEW YORK". UNIVERSITY ART MUSEUM, SANTA BARBARA CA, 1978.

RATCLIFF, CARTER: „VISIONARY IMAGES". THE RENAISSANCE SOCIETY AT THE UNIVERSITY OF CHICAGO, 1979.

„1979 BIENNIAL EXHIBITION". WHITNEY MUSEUM OF AMERICAN ART, NEW YORK, 1979.

YASSEN, ROBERT: „PAINTING AND SCULPTURE TODAY". INDIANAPOLIS MUSEUM OF ART, INDIANAPOLIS, 1980.

CATHCART, LINDA: „THE AMERICANS: THE LANDSCAPE". CONTEMPORARY ARTS MUSEUM, HOUSTON, 1981.

HUNTER, SAM: „NEW DIRECTIONS: CONTEMPORARY AMERICAN ART". THE COMMODITIESCORPORATION OF AMERICA, PRINCETON, 1981.

PLOUS, PHYLLIS: „CONTEMPORARY DRAWINGS: IN SEARCH OF AN IMAGE". UNIVERSITY ART MUSEUM, SANTA BARBARA, 1981.

„RECENT ACQUISITIONS: WORKS ON PAPER". HIGH MUSEUM, ATLANTA, 1981.

„35 ARTISTS RETURN TO ARTISTS SPACE. A BENEFIT EXHIBITION". ARTISTS SPACE, NEW YORK, 1981.

FERRULLI, HELEN AND YASSEN, ROBERT A.: „PAINTING AND SCULPTURE TODAY". INDIANAPOLIS MUSEUM OF ART, 1982.

GIMENEZ, CARMEN: „TENDENCIES IN NUEVA YORK". MINISTERIO DE CULTURA, MADRID, 1983.

WALKER, BARRY: „THE AMERICAN ARTIST AS PRINTMAKER". THE BROOKLYN MUSEUM, NEW YORK, 1983.

BATCHEN, GEOFFREY, ET AL.: „METAMANHATTAN". WHITNEY MUSEUM OF AMERICAN ART, DOWNTOWN BRANCH, NEW YORK, 1984.

FRIEDMAN, MARTIN, ET AL.: „IMAGES AND IMPRESSIONS: PAINTERS WHO PRINT". SULTAN ESSAY BY MARGE GOLDWATER. WALKER ART CENTER, MINNEAPOLIS, 1984.

KURKA, DON: „IMAGES ON PAPER INVITATIONAL". ART AND ARCHITECTURE GALLERY, UNIVERSITY OF TENNESSEE, KNOXVILLE, 1984.

KUROIWA, KYOSUKE, EDITOR: „PAINTING NOW". KITAKYUSHU MUNICIPAL MUSEUM OF ART, KIITAKYUSHU, 1984.

LEMIRE, SUZANNE AND MEILLEUR, MARTINE: „VIA NEW YORK". MUSEE D'ART CONTEMPORAIN, MONTREAL, 1984.

„DONALD SULTAN". GIAN ENZO SPERONE, ROME, 1985.

JONES, ALAN ET AL: „CORRESPONDENCES: NEW YORK ART NOW". LAFORET MUSEUM HARAJUKU, TOKYO, 1985.

NASGAARD, ROALD: „SELECTIONS FROM THE ROGER AND MYRA DAVIDSON COLLECTION OF INTERNATIONAL CONTEMPORARY ART". ART GALLERY OF ONTARIO, ONTARIO, 1986.

WALKER, BARRY: „PUBLIC AND PRIVATE. AMERICAN PRINTS TODAY. THE 24TH NATIONAL PRINT EXHIBITION". THE BROOKLYN MUSEUM, BROOKLYN, 1986.

COMBES, CHANTAL: „THE NEW ROMANTIC LANDSCAPE". THE WHITNEY MUSEUM OF AMERICAN ART, STAMFORD,CT, 1987.

DUNLOP, IAN AND WARREN, LYNNE: „DONALD SULTAN". MUSEUM OF CONTEMPORARY ART, CHICAGO, 1987.

„THE MONUMENTAL IMAGE". SONOMA STATE UNIVERSITY AT NORTHRIDGE, SONOMA CA, 1987.

„10 + 10: CONTEMPORARY SOVIET AND AMERICAN PAINTERS". HARRY N. ABRAMS, THE FORT WORTH ART ASSOCIATION, FORT WORTH, TX, 1989.

„DONALD SULTAN: WORKS ON PAPER". RUNKEL-HUE-WILLIAMS, LONDON, 1989.

„SEAN SCULLY/ DONALD SULTAN: ABSTRACTION/ REPRESENTATION". STANFORD UNIVERSITY MUSEUM OF ART, 1990.

LUEBBERS, LESLIE: „MIND AND MATTER: NEW AMERICAN ABSTRACTION". INTERNATIONAL ART PROJECT, WORLD PRINT COUNCIL, SAN FRANCISCO, 1990.

„DONALD SULTAN: PAINTINGS 1978-1992". ESSAY BY DONALD KUSPIT. GUILD HALL MUSEUM, EAST HAMPTON, NY, 1992.

„AN ODE TO GARDENS AND FLOWERS". ESSAY BY CONSTANCE SCHWARTZ. NASSAU COUNTY MUSEUM OF ART, ROSLYN HARBOR, NY, 1992.

WALKER, BARRY: „DONALD SULTAN: A PRINT RETROSPECTIVE". THE AMERICAN FEDERATION OF ARTS IN ASSOCIATION WITH RIZZOLI, NEW YORK, 1992.

WEINTRAUB, LINDA; DANTO, AUTHUR; MCEVILLEY, THOMAS: „ART ON THE EDGE AND OVER". ART INSIGHTS INC., LITCHFIELD, CT, 1996.

„VISUAL POETICS: THE ART OF MAMET, DAVID. BAR MITZVAH". TEXT BY MACKENZIE, MICHAEL, POEMS BY ROBERT CREELEY. MARCO FINE ARTS, EL SEGUNDO, CA., 1998.

„IN COMPANY: ROBERT CREELEY'S COLLABORATIONS". CASTELLANI MUSEUM OF NIAGRA UNIVERSITY/ WEATHERSPOON ART GALLERY. NIAGRA, NEW YORK, GREENSBORO, TAMPA, STANFORD, 1999.

MAMET, DAVID AND STEVEN HENRY MADOFF: „DONALD SULTAN. IN THE STILL-LIFE TRADITION". UNIVERSITY OF WASHINGTON PRESS, SEATTLE, WA., 1999.

„SPACE, ABSTRACTION AND FREEDOM". THE ACKLAND ART MUSEUM, CHAPEL HILL, NC, 2001.

SILVER, KENNETH E.: „MAKING PARADISE: ART, MODERNITY, AND THE MYTH OF THE FRENCH RIVIERA". THE MIT PRESS, CAMBRIDGE, MA, 2001.

BLAGG, MAX: „THE SMOKE RINGS". THE UNIVERSITY OF MICHIGAN MUSEUM OF ART, ANN ARBOR, MI, 2001.
„DIGITAL PRINTMAKING NOW". THE BROOKLYN MUSEUM OF ART, BROOKLYN, 2001.

SELECTION OF WORKS IN PUBLIC COLLECTIONS

The Ackland Art Museum, University of North Carolina, Chapel Hill
Addison Gallery of American Art, Andover, Massachusetts
Albright Knox Art Gallery, Buffalo, New York
The Arkansas Art Center, Little Rock
The Art Institute of Chicago, Illinois
Art Museum of Southeast Texas, Beaumont
Australian National Gallery, Canberra
Bank of America Corporation
Brooks Museum of Art, Memphis, Tennessee
Butler Institute of American Art , Youngstown, Ohio
Cincinnati Art Museum, Cincinnati, Ohio
Cleveland Art Museum, Cleveland, Ohio
Dallas Museum of Fine Arts, Texas
Denver Art Museum, Denver Colorado
Des Moines Art Center, Iowa
The Detroit Institute of Arts, Michigan
Fogg Art Museum, Harvard University, Cambridge, Massachusetts
The Hallmark Art Collection, Kansas City, Missouri
The High Museum of Art, Atlanta, Georgia
Hirshhorn Museum and Sculpture Garden, Washington, D.C.
Louise Wells Cameron Art Museum, Wilmington, North Carolina
Ludwig Museum, Budapest, Hungary
Kemper Museum of Contemporary Art & Design of the Kansas City Art Institute, Missouri
Kitakyushu Municipal Museum of Art, Tobataku Kitakyushu, Japan
The Metropolitan Museum of Art, New York
The Mint Museums, Charlotte, North Carolina
Modern Art Museum of Fort Worth, Texas
Modern Museum of Art, New York
Museum of Contemporary Art, San Diego, La Jolla, California
The Museum of Contemporary Art, Tokyo, Japan
The Museum of Fine Arts, Boston, Massachusetts
The Museum of Fine Arts, Houston, Texas
The Museum of Modern Art, New York
Nelson - Atkins Museum, Kansas City, Missouri
Neuberger Museum, State University of New York, Purchase
North Carolina Museum of Art, Raleigh, North Carolina
Palm Springs Art Museum, California
Pennsylvania Academy of the Fine Arts, Philadelphia
San Francisco Museum of Modern Art, California
Singapore Museum of Art, Singapore
Smith College, Museum of Art, Northampton, Massachusetts
The Solomon R. Guggenheim Museum, New York
The St. Louis Art Museum, Missouri
Tate Gallery, London
The Toledo Museum of Art, Ohio
Walker Art Center, Minneapolis, Minnesota
Whitney Museum of American Art, New York

Dots Sept 25 2009 Conté, charcoal and tempera on paper, 69 x 99 cm

IMPRESSUM

© Galerie Andres Thalmann, Zürich
© Abbildungen: Donald Sultan
© Foto: Bei den Fotografen
Übersetzung: Margret Powell-Joss
Gestaltung: Ruth Littman
Druck: werk zwei Print + Medien Konstanz GmbH, Konstanz
Auflage: 1000 Exemplare
ISBN: 978-3-9523571-0-1